LEON

Smoothies, Juices & Cocktails

NATURALLY FAST RECIPES

LEON

NATURALLY FAST RECIPES

Smoothies, Juices & Cocktails

By Henry Dimbleby, Kay Plunkett-Hogge, Claire Ptak & John Vincent

PHOTOGRAPHY BY GEORGIA GLYNN SMITH · DESIGN BY ANITA MANGAN

conran
OCTOPUS

Contents

Introduction 7

Smoothies & juices 10

Cocktails 24

Summer coolers 38

Winter warmers 50

Conversion chart 60

Index 62

Introduction

"Cheers." "Skol." "Your good health." There is a reason why we have different sayings for drinking. They mark an occasion. A morning ritual. A birthday. A rite of passage.

In this book, we have assembled the full family of liquid refreshment—a worldwide convention of drinks. Each with their own pin-on name card and information pack. From (sparkly) sandal-wearing smoothies to the sassiest of cocktails.

You will find the Leon Power Smoothie. (It won't help make you master of the universe—it's much better than that). You'll also find coolers for the summer, warmers for the winter, and a hot punch for Halloween.

We owe a debt of gratitude to the work of wider Leon friends (from the wider Leon family). They include "Uncle" Ian who, for a while, managed our restaurants and who's a charming and talented man. And to Tom Ward who is opening his own pork store. And Vince Jung who owns the Formosa Café in Hollywood, California, who has allowed us to put his Margarita in lights, and really big letters.

A manager of a soccer club once said that each time he wrote his team sheet he would get excited. That's how we feel about this collection of drinks. If we had them all in the locker rooms before kickoff we'd say: "We've been through a lot. We have trained hard. We've been up together at daybreak. We have been there for one another on our first dates. We are tasty as individuals. But we are most powerful as a team, so go out there and give everyone who has bought this book what they deserve. A drink for the darkest of early starts. A drink for the hottest of days. For the bitterest of winter days. For when they announce their engagement. For when they want to forgive or forget. Go out there and create magic."

We hope you feel the same. Cheers.

Henry & John

Basic Tools

Microplane zester

For getting the zest off citrus fruits. If you are using a traditional zester you will need to chopthe zest finely. Make sure you aren't so seduced by the microplane's easy action that you absentmindedly shred the white pith—it is very bitter.

Measuring spoons

Have one set and use them for everything. Whether this is superstition or not, we find that different sets seem to vary slightly.

Measuring cup

You can use a measuring cup to measure a rough quantity of liquids but, for many recipes, digital scales are useful for weighing liquids precisely. If you don't own a set of battery-operated digital scales they are widely available for $20.00 and up.

Speed peeler

Owning any other kind of peeler is a form of madness—a bit like when Björn Borg tried to make his comeback in professional tennis using a wooden racket. The speed peelers are by far the most effective.

Paring knife

For all those little jobs: e.g. freeing cakes from pans, trimming fruits, or scoring bread dough.

Juicer (or reamer)

Great for getting all the juice out of a small amount of fruit. Cheap, easy to clean, efficient, durable, beautiful, simple, and safe.

Immersion blender

For making fruit purees, seed milks, bringing chocolate and butter mixes back if they have split, and mixing flavors.

Ice cream machine

This is a complete luxury, because you can still make great ice cream without one. On the other hand, you could have a lot of fun with it and it saves time.

Bird's beak knife

A specialist knife for trimming fruit into particularly pleasing shapes.

Zester

For when you need a hit of zesty flavor and you are going to strain out the zest, for example, in a poaching liquid or ice cream base. You can also make delicate strands of candied zest by poaching them in a simple sugar syrup.

SMOOTHIES & JUICES

Energy Booster Smoothie

SERVES 4 • PREPARATION TIME: 5 MINUTES • COOKING TIME: NONE • ♥ WF GF DF V

The king of all smoothies. This bad boy (sorry, good boy—very good boy) is packed full of healthy omega-3 and is stuffed with all the vitamins in the alphabet. The secret weapon is avocado—one of nature's finest superfoods. As well as adding essential amino acids, it also brings a gorgeous creaminess to the smoothie.

1 **avocado**
2 handfuls EACH of any three of the following:
    hulled strawberries, **raspberries, blueberries,**
    blackberries, bilberries, loganberries
1 cup **orange juice**
1 tablespoon **flaxseed**, plain or toasted
2 ripe **bananas**

1. Pop everything into the blender—it's not an exact science, just toss 'em all in—and whizz until smooth.

TIPS

* When berries are in season, use them fresh—then freeze a load to use through the winter. Just put them straight into the blender, frozen, for a delicious chilled smoothie.

* Add soy milk instead of the orange juice if you like. If you do, add a splash of honey or agave syrup to replace the sweetness the orange juice provides.

Strawberry Power Smoothie

SERVES 2 • PREPARATION TIME: 5 MINUTES • COOKING TIME: NONE • ✓ WF GF V

When we introduced this to our menu, one of our regulars described it as "another small step for mankind."

1 small **banana**
a small handful of **fresh** or
  frozen strawberries
⅔ cup **rolled oats**
1 tablespoon **clear honey**
½ cup **Greek yogurt**
⅔ cup **whole milk**

TIPS

* If you can't get your
hands on fresh or
frozen strawberries, you
can add strawberry jam.

1. Peel the banana, and hull the strawberries.

2. Put all the ingredients into a blender and blend together.

Blackberry Power Smoothie

SERVES 2 • PREPARATION TIME: 5 MINUTES • COOKING TIME: NONE • ✓ WF GF V

We bring this onto the menu in fall, when it's getting a little late for strawberries.

1 small **banana**
a small handful of **fresh** or
  frozen blackberries
⅔ cup **rolled oats**
1 tablespoon **clear honey**
½ cup **Greek yogurt**
⅔ cup **whole milk**

TIPS

* If you can't get your
hands on fresh or
frozen blackberries, you
can add blackberry jam.

1. Peel the banana, and pick over the blackberries.

2. Put all the ingredients into a smoothie machine or a food processor and process them together.

OPPOSITE FROM TOP: CARROT, ORANGE & GINGER JUICE; STRAWBERRY POWER SMOOTHIE; GABRIELA'S GREEN SMOOTHIE; KIWI BREAKFAST SMOOTHIE; HATTIE'S SUPER-HEALTHY ALMOND SMOOTHIE; BLACKBERRY POWER SMOOTHIE.

Kiwi Breakfast Smoothie

SERVES 4 • PREPARATION TIME: 5 MINUTES • COOKING TIME: NONE • ♥ ✓ WF GF V

For those who don't like bananas, this smoothie makes a great substitute.

2 kiwis
a large handful of **berries** of your choice
1 teaspoon **flaxseeds**
1 teaspoon **sunflower seeds**
½ cup **Greek yogurt**
½ cup **fresh orange juice**

1. Peel the kiwis and wash the berries.

2. Put all the ingredients into a smoothie machine or a blender and process together until smooth.

Carrot, Orange & Ginger Juice

SERVES 2 • PREPARATION TIME: 5 MINUTES • COOKING TIME: NONE • ♥ ✓ WF GF DF V

A great cold-buster, this has become a regular on the Leon menu.

3 carrots
a thumb-sized piece of **fresh ginger**
2 cups freshly squeezed **orange juice**

1. Peel the carrots and the ginger.

2. Juice both in a juicing machine and pour into a large jug.

3. Add the freshly squeezed orange juice and mix well.

TIPS

* If you only have a carton of orange juice, this is a great way to pep it up.

Gabriela's Green Smoothie

SERVES 6 • PREPARATION TIME: 5 MINUTES • COOKING TIME: NONE • ♥ ✓ WF GF V

Gabriela is a friend of ours who specializes in raw food. This is not one for the faint-hearted. Some of us love it, for others it is inedible. It is made possible by the fact that raw kale is surprisingly sweet—try biting off a piece.

4 **kale leaves**, stems removed
1 cup **milk** or a dairy-free alternative,
    e.g. **rice milk**, **soy milk**, or **nut milk**
1 **banana**
1 **pear**
1 tablespoon **honey**
1 tablespoon **almond butter**
1 tablespoon **unsweetened cocoa powder**
    (or, for raw food fanatics, **cacao powder**)

TIPS

* If you can't find almond butter, use peanut butter.

1. Start by blending the kale with the milk and ⅔ cup of water until there are no more chunks.

2. Add the rest of the ingredients and blend well.

Hattie's Superhealthy Almond Smoothie

SERVES 2 • PREPARATION TIME: 5 MINUTES • COOKING TIME: NONE • ♥ WF DF GF V

And for those who are looking for something dairy free…

1 **kiwi**
1 medium **banana**
2 large handfuls of **berries**—
    whatever is in season
8 **almonds**, skins on

2 heaping tablespoons
rolled oats
1 tablespoon **pumpkin seeds**
1 tablespoon **sunflower seeds**
1 cup **rice milk**, **almond milk**,
    or **soy milk**

1. Peel the kiwi and the banana. Wash the berries.

2. Put all the ingredients into a smoothie machine or a blender and process together until smooth.

Cucumber Cooler

This might just be the most beautiful-looking drink in the world, and it's refreshing too.

1 **cucumber**
1 **lime**
6½ cups **cold water**

1. Peel the cucumber, discarding the peel. Then, still using the peeler, keep peeling the flesh into long ribbons, turning it as you work. Drop the cucumber ribbons straight into your favorite jug, and keep making more until you get to the seeds.

2. Squeeze in the juice of the lime, and add the water and plenty of ice.

Melon Fizz

1 ripe **cantaloupe melon**
juice of 2 **limes**
4 cups **cold sparkling water**

1. Peel the melon and remove the seeds. Chop the flesh and blend it in a food processor with the juice of 1 lime.

2. Pour through a fine strainer into a wide-necked pitcher or bowl, squeezing as much of the juice through as you can.

3. Fill up with sparkling water and serve.

OPPOSITE FROM LEFT: SPARKLING STRAWBERRY COOLER; CUCUMBER COOLER; MELON FIZZ.

Toph's Strawberryade

SERVES 2 • PREPARATION TIME: 5 MINUTES• COOKING TIME: NONE • WF GF V

¾ cup **water** or **sparkling water**
1–2 tablespoons **agave syrup** (depending how sweet
you like it—I like it tart, so I just use 1 tablespoon)
¼ cup **lemon juice** (about 2 lemons)
5–6 **strawberries**, hulled and chopped

1. Blend all of the above together (add a little ice if you wish, but if you do, then drop the water).

Sparkling Strawberry Cooler

MAKES: 6 CUPS • PREPARATION TIME: 2 MINUTES• COOKING TIME: NONE • ♥ ✓ WF GF DF V

1 pint **strawberries**
6 **mint leaves**
juice of 1 **lemon**
2 tablespoons **honey**
4 cups **cold sparkling water**

1. Process everything except the water in a blender.

2. Add ice to the blender if you wish.

3. Transfer to a pitcher, stir in the sparkling water, and serve.

Watermelon Slurpie

SERVES 2–4 • PREPARATION TIME: 10 MINUTES • COOKING TIME: NONE • ♥ WF GF V

All over Thailand, you see carts advertising *ponlamai puun* or "spun fruit." These icy cool fruit drinks come in myriad flavors—perfect for the tropical heat. Our favorite is the watermelon—pink, refreshing, and sweet.

> 1 smallish ripe **watermelon** (4½–6½ lbs), peeled,
>   seeded, and diced, preferably chilled
> ½ teaspoon **salt**
> a few **ice cubes**
> 2 tablespoons **simple syrup** (see page 32)

1. Blend the watermelon in a blender with the salt and ice cubes. Only add the simple syrup if the watermelon is not sweet enough.

TIPS

* To be very Thai you could finish the slurpie off with a spoonful or two of sweetened condensed milk or some coconut milk.
* Add a few fresh mint leaves and a squeeze of lime.

Date Shake

SERVES 2–4 • PREPARATION TIME: 5 MINUTES • COOKING TIME: NONE • WF GF V

> 15 **whole dates**, pitted and coarsely chopped
> 1 cup unsweetened **soy milk**
> 1 ripe **banana**, peeled and chopped
> 2–4 **ice cubes**
> a pinch of **ground cinnamon** or **ground cardamom**

1. Put everything into a blender and blend on high power until it's really well blended, thick, and creamy. Pour and serve immediately.

TIPS

* You could use whole milk or skim milk, or rice milk— it's up to you.
* Try replacing the banana with a scoop of good vanilla ice cream or another handful of pitted dates.

COCKTAILS

Soul Fruit Cup

Our friend Giles runs his own company called Soul Shakers, traveling the world making cocktails at some of the best parties in the world (lucky boy). He put together a cocktail bar for the Regatta (a British rowing event) and served this drink as his version of Pimm's. Perfect to sip on a hot summer's day, while others work up a sweat.

½ cup **gin**
⅓ cup **Campari**
½ cup **sweet vermouth**
⅔ cup **pink grapefruit juice**
juice of 2 **lemons**
6–8 slices of **cucumber**
lemonade (homemade or bottled)
strawberries and **mint**, to garnish (optional)

1. Pour the alcohol, grapefruit juice, and lemon juice into a pitcher.

2. Add the cucumber and lemonade and stir.

3. Pour into iced glasses and garnish with strawberries and/or mint if you desire.

Leon Summer Punch

SERVES 6 • PREPARATION TIME: 5 MINUTES • COOKING TIME: NONE • WF GF V

Think summer, all your best friends, your backyard, a balmy evening, and a victory in your favorite ball game.

16 **strawberries**
2 **pears** (nice and ripe)
⅔ cup **simple syrup** (see page 32)
⅔ cup **vodka**
½ cup **lemon juice**
bottle of **prosecco**

1. Blend the strawberries and pears to make a simple puree, adding the simple syrup to sweeten.

2. Add the puree to a pitcher and stir in the vodka and lemon juice.

3. Fill up with prosecco and stir. Pour into champagne flutes and propose a toast.

The Rude Boi

SERVES 1 • PREPARATION TIME: 2 MINUTES • COOKING TIME: NONE • WF GF V

Here's a tropical-inspired nonalcoholic cocktail for the kids, which we invented for Kay's nephews Alex and Alastair when they were younger. The high point in its genesis was the time Alastair discovered the cocktail shaker, and that carbonated drinks don't respond well to shaking, all in the same afternoon.

ice
store-bought mango and
   passion fruit smoothie
ginger beer

TIPS

* You can substitute the ginger beer for sparkling pineapple and grapefruit drink if you prefer.

1. Fill a Collins glass with ice. Pour in 1 measure of the mango and passion fruit smoothie. Fill up with ginger beer. Stir to blend and serve at once.

The Spritz

SERVES 2 • PREPARATION TIME: 2 MINUTES • COOKING TIME: NONE • WF GF V

The Venetian drink of choice. It's cool, bittersweet, and colorful—just what you need for a party.

a dash of **Aperol** or **Campari**
   per glass
1–1¼ cups **prosecco** (or white
   wine and sparkling water)
a small bowl of **ice**

2 chunks of **orange** (preferably
   blood orange)
2 **green olives** in brine, rinsed

1. Pour a dash of Aperol or Campari into each glass.

2. Fill up to about halfway with the prosecco or white wine and sparkling water. Add an ice cube.

3. Spear an orange chunk and an olive on each of 2 long toothpicks and place one in each glass. Serve with the bowl of ice on the side.

FROM LEFT: THE RUDE BOI; THE SPRITZ; VINCE JUNG'S MARGARITA.

Vince Jung's Margarita

SERVES 1 • PREPARATION TIME: 2 MINUTES • COOKING TIME: NONE • WF GF V

Kay's friend Vince is the third-generation owner of the landmark Hollywood bar, the Formosa Café, which has been serving everyone from movie stars to hoodlums since... well... it depends on who you talk to, but no one's really sure. Vince's margaritas are the business.

¼ cup **silver tequila**
2 tablespoons **Cointreau**
the juice from 1½ **limes**
3 tablespoons **simple syrup** (see below)

1. Fill a metal cocktail shaker with ice and add all the ingredients. Shake briskly. Serve on the rocks or straight up in a salt-rimmed glass, and garnish with a wedge of lime.

Simple Syrup

A cocktail staple, this is supereasy to make and will see you through countless margaritas and other cocktails.

½ cup **superfine sugar**
½ cup **water**

1. Mix the sugar and water together in a saucepan over low to medium heat until the sugar has completely dissolved. Don't boil.

2. Once it's all dissolved, set the saucepan aside to cool, then decant the syrup into a screw-top jar or bottle with a securely fitting lid and store until you need it.

TIPS

* Be sure to sterilize your jar or bottle first.

* Simple syrup is also now available to buy in bottles at some supermarkets.

Kamomilla Fizz

This is a slightly more taxing drink, for those of you who see yourselves as cocktail connoisseurs. It was invented for the International Finlandia Vodka Cup in 2006. It won the best long drink and we served bucketloads at the Big Chill the same year. The camomile and cucumber work beautifully together, and it's a great long summer drink. You can substitute the vodka with gin, which also works really well (it's known as a 10cc).

> 3 slices of **cucumber** (each about ⅛ inch thick)
> ½ a **lemon**, cut into 4 wedges
> 5 teaspoons **camomile tea syrup** (see below)
> 2½ tablespoons **vodka**
> **ice**
> **sparkling water** or **club soda**

1. In a cocktail shaker, muddle the cucumber and 3 of the lemon wedges with the camomile tea syrup. Muddle it quite hard to work the juice and oil out of the lemon.

2. Add the vodka and ice and shake for a good 10 seconds. Strain into an ice-filled highball glass.

3. Top with sparkling water or soda. Garnish with the remaining lemon wedge. Kippis!

Camomile Tea Syrup

Make a strong brew of camomile tea—about 3 teabags in 1 cup of hot water. Leave it to stand for 5 minutes. Remove the teabags and add 1 cup of superfine sugar, then stir until the sugar has dissolved and let cool.

Champagne Cocktail

SERVES 1 • PREPARATION TIME: 2 MINUTES • COOKING TIME: NONE • ♥ ✓ WF GF DF V

The drink with which to toast the New Year.

Angostura bitters
1 sugar cube
brandy
Champagne

1. Shake a couple of drops of Angostura onto the sugar cube and put it into the bottom of a Champagne glass.

2. Pour on a little brandy. It is meant to be just a dash, but they say that fortune favors the bold.

3. Fill up the glass with Champagne.

TIPS

* You can use cava or prosecco or any dry sparkling white wine instead of Champagne (we normally do).

* If you don't like brandy, you can omit it. The original recipe doesn't include it.

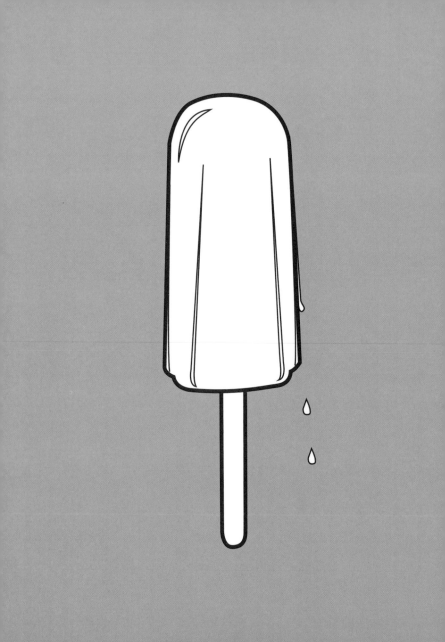

SUMMER COOLERS

Fabulous Ice Pop

PREPARATION TIME: 10 MINUTES • FREEZING TIME: OVERNIGHT (MINIMUM 2½ HOURS) • ♥ ✓ WF DF GF V

Three grown-up ice pops to cool you down on a hot summer's day. Each recipe makes pops for 6—you just need to pick which flavor to make first.

Strawberry Ice Pops

♥ ✓ WF DF GF V

2 pints **strawberries**, hulled
3 level teaspoons **fructose**
1 tablespoon **vodka**

Mango Ice Pops

♥ ✓ WF DF GF V

12 cups **mango flesh** (from 13 large mangoes)
3 level teaspoons **fructose**
1 tablespoon **vodka**

Baileys Ice Pops

✓ WF GF V

2 cups **heavy cream**
3 level teaspoons **fructose**
3 tablespoons **Baileys**

1. Put all the ingredients into a blender and blend until smooth.

2. Divide equally between ice pop molds and push in the sticks (or cut-off straws).

3. Put in the freezer until firm.

TIPS

* The vodka brings out the flavor of the fruit. Leave the alcohol out if you want to avoid sedating your children.

* Create a rocket ship (see opposite). This is time-consuming but rewarding. Freeze each of these ice pops in individual layers one after the other. Then drizzle a little melted chocolate on top (make sure the ice pop is *really* cold first), and sprinkle on some space dust or sherbet. Cool on a sheet of wax paper in the freezer.

Champagne Granita

SERVES 4–6 • PREPARATION TIME: 10 MINUTES • FREEZING TIME: 3-4 HOURS • ♥ WF GF DF V

A lovely light way to end a meal. Or, if you are feeling extravagant, to serve as a palate cleanser between the appetizer and the main course.

½ cup **superfine sugar**
1 cup **water**
1⅓ **Champagne** (½ a bottle)
juice of 1 **lemon**

1. Dissolve the sugar and water together in a saucepan over moderate heat. Stir in the Champagne. Add lemon juice to taste.

2. Freeze in a roasting pan or other container that is shallow and wide, but will fit into your freezer. Every 30 minutes, use a whisk to stir and break up the ice that has formed, until all the liquid has turned into paper-thin ice shards.

We originally wanted to do an absinthe granita, one that would make a party swing. Sadly the stuff was so alcoholic that we couldn't get it to freeze, leaving us with a lethal, ice-cold absinthe syrup. Best to stick to Champagne really.

CLAIRE

TIPS

* You can play around with granitas as much as you want. Sharp rosé wine and fruit work well together, as do coffee, and vodka.

* Different alcohols also go well with different fruits. The alcohol can really bring out the flavor of a fruit, lifting it and making it more complex. Try Grand Marnier with orange, kirsch with cherries or pineapple. There are some wonderful small distilleries appearing that are mixing fruits and alcohol. You can find pear, greengage, quince, and others. They are worth seeking out.

OPPOSITE TOP: CHAMPAGNE GRANITA, LEFT: QUINCE GRANITA, RIGHT: CLEMENTINE GRANITA.

Clementine Granita

SERVES 4–6 • PREPARATION TIME: 5 MINUTES • COOKING TIME: 10 MINUTES • ♥ WF GF DF V

A light, fruity granita for winter refreshment.

½ cup **water**
¼ cup **superfine sugar**
1¼ cups **clementine juice**, strained

1. Combine the water and sugar over low heat to make a syrup. Cool completely.

2. Stir in the strained clementine juice.

3. Freeze in a roasting pan or other container that is shallow and wide, but will fit into your freezer. Every 30 minutes, use a whisk to stir and break up the ice that has formed, until all the liquid has turned into paper-thin ice shards.

TIPS

* Serve with grapefruit or orange sections, in pretty glass cups.

* It is also nice with a crisp buttery cookie.

Quince Granita

SERVES 4–6 • PREPARATION TIME: 25 MINUTES • COOKING TIME: 2 HOURS
FREEZING TIME: 5 HOURS • ♥ WF GF DF V

A more scented, full-bodied granita, and a lovely way to finish off an cool evening.

1½ **quinces**
1½ cups **superfine sugar**
3 cups **water**
1 **vanilla bean**, split in half lengthwise
juice of ½ a **lemon**

1. Peel and quarter the quinces. Put the sugar, water, and vanilla bean into a saucepan and stir to dissolve the sugar. Bring to a boil.

2. Add the quinces and the lemon juice. Simmer for 1–2 hours, or until the quinces are tender when pierced and rosy in color.

3. Remove the quinces from the syrup and core them. Remove the vanilla bean.

4. Puree the quinces and syrup together, then add some water to adjust the consistency so it's less thick.

5. Freeze in a roasting pan or other container that is shallow and wide, but will fit into your freezer. Every 30 minutes, use a whisk to stir and break up the ice that has formed, until all the liquid has turned into paper-thin ice shards.

TIPS

* Quinces are thick and fluffy when pureed and lend themselves very well to being frozen. Be sure to cook them long enough so that they are tender.

* Add a teaspoon or two of honey to the puree as a variation. Honey and quince have an affinity for each other.

Apple Sorbet

SERVES 4–6 • PREPARATION TIME: 25 MINUTES • FREEZING TIME: UP TO 5 HOURS • ♥ WF GF DF V

We call this apple sorbet, but apple snow might be a better description. It is light and fluffy and pure as the driven…. The egg white and gelatin add protein, which gives the sorbet its gorgeous texture.

2 cups **apple cider**
¼ cup **superfine sugar**
1 teaspoon **powdered gelatin**
1 **egg white**
a splash of **apple brandy** (optional)

1. Gently heat 1 cup of the apple cider with the sugar in a small saucepan.

2. In another pan, soften the gelatin with the remaining apple cider before heating it gently to dissolve. Once dissolved, combine the two liquids and pour into a container to cool. When cooled, place in the refridgerator until ready to freeze.

3. Whisk the egg white to soft peaks and fold it into the chilled sorbet base. Add the apple brandy, if using, then pour into an ice cream machine and freeze according to the manufacturer's instructions.

TIPS

* Use a high-quality, tart apple cider, or, even better, juice your own apples.

* Try substituting pear, peach, watermelon, or grape juice for the apple. If they are very sweet you might need a squeeze of lemon to add some acidity.

Blood Orange & White Wine Gelatin

SERVES 6 • PREPARATION TIME: 10 MINUTES
COOKING TIME: 10 MINUTES • ♥ WF GF DF (V IF YOU USE VEGETARIAN GELATIN)

There is something about the limpid tremble of a lightly set gelatin that is devilishly alluring. This one is based on a recipe from Richard Olney's 1970 classic *The French Menu Cookbook*. His recipe includes instructions on how to make the gelatin by boiling calves' feet. Thankfully we can now buy perfectly good gelatin (from animal sources or vegetarian) in pristine transparent sheets.

⅔ cup **sweet white wine** (e.g. Muscat or Baumes de Venise)
¼ cup **superfine sugar**
1 stick of **cinnamon**
2 cups fresh **blood orange juice** (5 or 6 oranges)
4 leaves of **gelatin** (about 4 teaspoons)

1. Put the wine into a pan with the sugar, the cinnamon stick, and ⅔ cup of the orange juice. Bring to a boil, then remove from the heat and discard the cinnamon stick. Melt the gelatin into the juice (following the package instructions).

2. Pour the rest of the orange juice into a large measuring jug or pitcher and add the liquid from the saucepan. Stir thoroughly, then pour into your mold. Let cool, then put into the refridgerator until set.

3. To turn out, loosen the edges of the gelatin gently with your fingers. Dip the base of the mold into a bowl of hot water for 1–2 seconds, place a plate on top, then invert the mold and shake. Serve with light or heavy cream.

TIPS

*   Richard Olney uses orange and lemon juice rather than blood orange juice. You can experiment with all kinds of liquids: white wines, pomegranate juice, grapefruit juice, and lime juice are all good.

*   Try flavoring the gelatin with herbs and spices—rosemary with orange, for example, or cardamom with coconut milk.

*   We prefer a lighter set. Use less gelatin where you can get away with it.

*   Try putting whole fruit inside your gelatin (grapes, plum slices, strawberries, raspberries, etc.). You can make the fruit float if you set a layer of gelatine first, then add the fruit followed by the rest of the gelatin.

*   Some fruits have enzymes that digest gelatin, which will make it difficult to set. These include: figs, kiwis, mango, melon, papaya, peach, and pineapple. Fresh ginger also has this effect.

WINTER WARMERS

Hot Chocolate 5 Ways

SERVES 1 • PREPARATION TIME: 2 MINUTES • COOKING TIME: 10 MINUTES • V

Warming and reassuring, it's a hug in a mug. Here are our top five:

The Building Block Choc

The basic hot chocolate from which all the others (in this book) descend.

1 mug of **milk**
1 oz **good-quality semisweet chocolate**, grated

1. Heat the milk gently in a small saucepan. As soon as it reaches scalding point but before it boils, whisk in the grated chocolate until it has all melted thoroughly into the milk. (This has the added bonus of frothing everything up a bit.)

2. Pour into your mug and serve.

Mexican Hot Chocolate

Add a stick of **cinnamon**, a good grating of **orange zest**, and a pinch of **chile powder** to give your chocolate a South of the Border feel. Arriba!

Swedish Hot Chocolate

Adults Only…well, you know what we mean…add a good slug of **vodka** and put an Abba track on the stereo.

Natasha & Eleanor's Hot Chocolate

Top the Building Block Choc with a good sprinkling of **miniature marshmallows** and plenty of **whipped cream**.

Jamaican Hot Chocolate

Stir it up with a good pinch of freshly ground **allspice** and a slug of **Jamaican rum**. Now we be chillin'.

TIPS

* We're using a good semisweet chocolate here so we can avoid all the added sugar, etc., you'll find in powdered cocoa mix.

* All recipes these days talk about "good-quality chocolate." They'll then go on to specify a minimum of cocoa solids in the chocolate, and so on. In this case, the flavor of the chocolate absolutely determines the flavor of your hot chocolate, so buy the brand you like. We love Original Beans—for their flavor, of course, but also for their fantastic work in the conservation of threatened rain forests and promotion of sustainable farming practices.

Hot Halloween Punch

SERVES ABOUT 20 • PREPARATION TIME: NONE • COOKING TIME: 10 MINUTES • V

It was Halloween 2009, and Giles and I were at a party at the "Lady Castle" in London (a big house full of beautiful, single girls). Giles had the idea of making a hot punch—it was freezing outside. We used various odds and ends that he found in the kitchen and came up with this. The party went with a swing, and this concoction is now a must every Hallowe'en.

1¾ cups **brandy**
6½ cups **hard dry cider**
⅔ cup **sugar**
1¼ cups **lemon juice**
10 dashes of **Angostura bitters**
2–3 **cinnamon sticks**
5–6 **cloves**
lemon zest, to garnish

1. Pour all the ingredients except the lemon zest into a large saucepan and bring to a slow simmer.

2. Ladle into heatproof glasses and garnish with a twist of lemon zest.

Christmas Cocktail

SERVES I • PREPARATION TIME: 2 MINUTES • COOKING TIME: NONE • GF DF V

I first drank this in a fashionable Soho bar in London and realized immediately that my mom would love it. I made it last Christmas for the family. My mom did love it. Dad drank far too much of it. Substitute berry syrup for Campari and use club soda instead of prosecco, and the kids can join in, too.

½ cup **Campari**
¼ cup **lemon juice**
½ cup **clementine juice**
¼ cup **simple syrup** (see recipe page 32)
1¾ cups **prosecco**
orange zest, to garnish

1. In a cocktail shaker combine the Campari, lemon juice, clementine juice, and sugar syrup.

2. Add ice and shake.

3. Strain the mixture equally into 6 champagne glasses and fill up with prosecco. Garnish with a twist of orange zest.

Glögg

SERVES 10–12 • STEEPING TIME: 2–4 HOURS • HEATING TIME: 20 MINUTES • V

Kay got this recipe from her mom and dad, who in turn got it from Scandinavian friends in Bangkok back in the day…. It will certainly make a Christmas party go with a swing!

1 bottle of **vodka**
1 bottle of **red wine**
5 **cardamom pods,** cracked open
5 **cloves**
1 **stick of cinnamon**
1 piece of **orange rind**
1 piece of **fresh ginger**
1–1½ cups **sugar** (or to taste)
peeled **almonds** and **raisins**—a big handful of each, to serve

1. Mix all the ingredients and leave for 2–4 hours.

2. Heat the Glögg slowly. Do not boil.

3. Add the almonds and raisins just before serving.

Irish Coffee

SERVES 4 • PREPARATION TIME: 15 MINUTES • COOKING TIME: NONE • WF GF V

Smooth and creamy, a proper Irish coffee is deeply warming and sinfully delicious.

freshly brewed **hot coffee** (enough for 4)
4 teaspoons **brown sugar**
½ cup **Irish whiskey**
1 cup **heavy cream**, very lightly whipped
4 **Irish coffee glass mugs**

1. Make a fresh pot of coffee.

2. Place a teaspoon of brown sugar in the bottom of each Irish coffee mug and then pour in the hot coffee, leaving about 1 inch of room at the top of the mug. Stir gently.

3. Add 2 tablespoons of Irish whiskey to each mug.

4. Pour the barely whipped cream over the back of a spoon and into the mug.

TIPS

* The sugar and alcohol both help the cream to float on top, creating the look of a pint of Guinness, so do not omit them.

* The idea is that you sip the Irish coffee slowly through the cream, so it is important that the cream is not too stiff.

Vodka Espresso

SERVES I • PREPARATION TIME: I MINUTE • COOKING TIME: NONE • V

This drink has been a favorite of the London bar scene since the mid-nineties. Rumor has it that its birthplace was the Pharmacy—the artist Damien Hirst's now defunct joint in Notting Hill. An experienced barman can tell how many of these caffeine-loaded cocktails a customer has had from the twitching in the arm or the judder of the head. Be warned: after three it is almost impossible to sit down.

> 2½ tablespoons **vodka**
> 1 tablespoon **Kahlúa**
> 2 tablespoons **espresso**
> **superfine sugar**
> **coffee beans**, to garnish (optional)

1. In a cocktail shaker combine the vodka, Kahlúa, espresso, and a pinch of sugar (it's up to you how sweet you like it). Pack it full of ice and shake it really hard for about 10 seconds: you want a nice froth on top, so shake it thoroughly.

2. Pour into a martini glass or champagne flute and garnish with 3 coffee beans if you have them.

3. This recipe is for one cocktail. You can probably fit two in one shaker, but any more than that and you'll lose the lovely crème on the top.

CONVERSION CHART FOR COMMON MEASURES

LIQUIDS

15 ml	$1/2$ fl oz
25 ml	1 fl oz
50 ml	2 fl oz
75 ml	3 fl oz
100ml	3 $1/2$ fl oz
125 ml	4 fl oz
150 ml	$1/4$ pint
175 ml	6 fl oz
200 ml	7 fl oz
250 ml	8 fl oz
275 ml	9 fl oz
300 ml	$1/2$ pint
325 ml	11 fl oz
350 ml	12 fl oz
375 ml	13 fl oz
400 ml	14 fl oz
450 ml	$3/4$ pint
475 ml	16 fl oz
500 ml	17 fl oz
575 ml	18 fl oz
600 ml	1 pint
750 ml	1 $1/4$ pints
900 ml	1 $1/2$ pints
1 liter	1 $3/4$ pints
1.2 liters	2 pints
1.5 liters	2 $1/2$ pints
1.8 liters	3 pints
2 liters	3 $1/2$ pints
2.5 liters	4 pints
3.6 liters	6 pints

WEIGHTS

5 g	$1/4$ oz
15 g	$1/2$ oz
20 g	$3/4$ oz
25 g	1 oz
50 g	2 oz
75 g	3 oz
125 g	4 oz
150 g	5 oz
175 g	6 oz
200 g	7 oz
250 g	8 oz
275 g	9 oz
300 g	10 oz
325 g	11 oz
375 g	12 oz
400 g	13 oz
425 g	14 oz
475 g	15 oz
500 g	1 lb
625 g	1 $1/4$ lb
750 g	1 $1/2$ lb
875 g	1 $3/4$ lb
1 kg	2 lb
1.25 kg	2 $1/2$ lb
1.5 kg	3 lb
1.75 kg	3 $1/2$ lb
2 kg	4 lb

MEASUREMENTS

5 mm	1/4 inch
1 cm	1/2 inch
1.5 cm	3/4 inch
2.5 cm	1 inch
5 cm	2 inches
7 cm	3 inches
10 cm	4 inches
12 cm	5 inches
15 cm	6 inches
18 cm	7 inches
20 cm	8 inches
23 cm	9 inches
25 cm	10 inches
28 cm	11 inches
30 cm	12 inches
33 cm	13 inches

Key to Symbols/Nutritional Info

♥	LOW SATURATED FATS
✓	LOW GLYCEMIC (GI) LOAD
WF	WHEAT FREE
GF	GLUTEN FREE
DF	DAIRY FREE
V	VEGETARIAN
🐦 TIPS	COOKING TIPS, EXTRA INFORMATION, AND ALTERNATIVE IDEAS

Index

A

almonds 14, 17, 57
Angostura bitters 37, 54
Aperol 30
apple sorbet 46–7
avocado, in smoothie 12–13

B

Baileys, ice pops 40
bananas
    date shake 22
    in smoothies 12–13, 15, 17
berries 12–13, 15, 16, 17, 48
bilberries 12
blackberries 12, 14–15
blueberries 12
brandy 37, 46, 54

C

camomile tea syrup 33
Campari 28, 30, 56
carrot, orange & ginger juice 14, 16
champagne 36–7, 42–3
cherries, granita 43
chocolate, hot 52–3
Christmas drinks 56, 57
cider 54
clementines 42, 44, 56
cocktails
    champagne 36–7
    Christmas 56
    Kamomilla fizz 33
    Leon summer punch 29
    margarita 31, 32
    the Rude Boi 30–1
    Soul fruit cup 28
    the Spritz 30–1
    vodka espresso 59
coffee 43, 58, 59
Cointreau 32
conversion charts 60–1
cucumber 18–19, 28, 33

D

date shake 22, 23

G

gin 28, 33
ginger beer 30
Glögg 57
Grand Marnier 43
granitas 42–3, 44, 45
grapefruit juice 28, 48
grapes 46, 48

H

Halloween punch 54–5
honey 12, 15, 17, 21, 45
hot drinks
    chocolate 52–3
    Glögg 57
    Halloween punch 54–5
    Irish coffee 58

I

ice pops 40–1
Irish coffee 58

J

jelly, orange & white wine 48
juices
    carrot, orange & ginger 14, 16
    cucumber cooler 18–19
    melon fizz 18–19
    strawberry cooler 19, 21
    watermelon slurpie 22–3
Jung, Vince, margarita 31, 32

K

Kahlúa 59
kale 17
key to symbols 61
kirsch 43
kiwis 14, 16, 17, 48

L

lemon juice 21, 28, 29, 33, 43, 45, 48, 54, 56
limes 18–19, 32, 48
loganberries 12

M

mango 30, 40, 48
margarita 31, 32
measurements 61
melon 48
    cantaloupe fizz 18–19
    watermelon 22–3, 46

O

Olney, Richard 48
orange juice
    blood orange & white wine gelatin 48–9
    carrot, & ginger 14, 16
    granita 43
    in smoothies 12–13, 16

P

passion fruit 30
peach 46, 48
pears 17, 29, 46
pineapple 43, 48
prosecco 29, 30, 37, 56
punch
    Halloween 54–5
    Leon summer 29

Q

quince granita 42, 45

R

raspberries, in smoothies 12
rice milk 17, 22
rolled oats, in smoothies 15, 17
rum 52

S

seeds 12, 16, 17
smoothie
    blackberry power 15
    date shake 22, 23
    energy booster 12–13
    Gabriela's green 14, 17
    Hattie's superhealthy almond 14, 17
    kiwi breakfast 14, 16
    strawberry power 15
sorbet 46–7
soy milk 12, 17, 22
strawberries
    in gelatin 48
    ice pops 40
    Leon summer punch 29
    in smoothies 12, 14–15
    sparkling cooler 19, 21
    Toph's strawberryade 21, 23
syrup 32, 33

T

tequila 32

V

vermouth, sweet 28
vodka 29, 33, 40, 43, 52, 57, 59

W

watermelon
    slurpie 22–3
    sorbet 46
weights and measures 60–1
whiskey, Irish 58
wine
    red/rosé 43, 57
    sparkling 29, 30, 36–7, 42–3, 56
    white 48–9

Y

yogurt, in smoothies 15, 16

First published in Great Britain in 2013 by Conran Octopus Limited,
a part of Octopus Publishing Group,
Endeavour House, 189 Shaftesbury Avenue, London WC2H 8JY
www.octopusbooks.co.uk

An Hachette UK Company
www.hachette.co.uk

Distributed in the US by Hachette Book Group USA
237 Park Avenue, New York NY 10017 USA

Distributed in Canada by Canadian Manda Group
165 Dufferin Street, Toronto, Ontario, Canada M6K 3H6

Publisher: Alison Starling
Senior Editor: Sybella Stephens
Assistant Editor: Stephanie Milner
Art Director: Jonathan Christie
Art Direction, Design and Illustrations: Anita Mangan
Design Assistant: Abigail Read
Photography: Georgia Glynn Smith
Production Manager: Katherine Hockley

ISBN 978 1 84091 631 7

Printed in China

A note from the authors...
We have endeavored to be as accurate as possible in all the preparation and cooking times
listing in the recipes in this book. However they are an estimate based on our own timings
during recipe testing, and should be taken as a guide only, not as the literal truth. We have
also tried to source all our food facts carefully. However, we are not scientists, so our food facts
and nutrition advice are not absolute. If you feel you require consultation with a nutritionist,
consult your family doctor or healthcare provider for a recommendation.